3 4028 09269 2509
HARRIS COUNTY PUBLIC LIBRARY

J 551.5 Des
De Seve, Karen
Little kids first big book of weather
WITHDRAWN
$14.99
ocn971247877
1st edition.

W9-AQZ-607

LITTLE KIDS FIRST BIG BOOK OF WEATHER

KAREN DE SEVE

NATIONAL GEOGRAPHIC KiDS

WASHINGTON, D.C.

CONTENTS

CHAPTER FIVE

CHAPTER SIX

CHAPTER SEVEN

INTRODUCTION

If you are wondering about the weather, you have come to the right place! This book turns weather inside out to reveal how different weather conditions happen. Each chapter explores a different type of weather that is probably happening somewhere on Earth right now. The end of the book shares details about how we understand and forecast the weather, and also how weather is related to—but not the same as—climate.

CHAPTER ONE introduces the notion of weather and how weather changes around the world. Lively images and call-outs invite readers to think about and enjoy the weather where they live. At the end of this chapter—and every other chapter—a fun game reinforces the ideas that were just covered.

CHAPTER TWO describes hot weather. Find out why some places on Earth are hotter than others, and learn how to stay cool and safe when the heat hits.

CHAPTER THREE explores windy weather. From gentle breezes to fierce windstorms, you will see how wind and the world shape each other.

CHAPTER FOUR investigates clouds from top to bottom, describing how and why they form.

CHAPTER FIVE describes rainy weather, from rain clouds to raindrops to rainstorms.

CHAPTER SIX opens the door on cold weather. You'll uncover why it gets cold in some places, how water freezes, and why winter storms form.

CHAPTER SEVEN explains how scientists study the weather so that people can prepare for what is coming.

HOW TO USE THIS BOOK

COLORFUL PHOTOGRAPHS illustrate each spread, supporting the text and showcasing the different types of weather around the world.

INTERACTIVE QUESTIONS in each section encourage conversations related to the topics.

POP-UP FACTS sprinkled throughout provide added information about the weather.

PARENT TIPS in the back of the book provide fun activity suggestions that relate to weather.

A GAME at the end of each chapter reinforces concepts covered in that section.

A GLOSSARY on the final pages provides definitions for key terms found throughout the text.

CHAPTER 1

WONDERFUL WEATHER

Each day, the air feels different when you step outside. That is the weather. Get ready to explore how weather happens and how it changes—by the minute, hour, and day!

THE WEATHER OUTSIDE

Look outside. Is it raining or is the sun shining? Maybe the wind is blowing. Sunny, rainy, and windy are all different types of weather. The weather changes each day. In fact, it can change many times during a single day.

Weather is also different around the world. It might be cloudy at your house and sunny many miles away. Let's discover what makes the weather!

What is your favorite kind of weather?

Pictures from space, like this one, show where storms are happening.

WEATHER always happens in **THE AIR.**

No clouds means sunny weather.

Spinning clouds mean a bad storm is in the sky.

HOW WEATHER HAPPENS

The Earth heats up each day and cools down each night. When the sun rises in the morning, sunlight warms the chilly ground. Soon, the warm ground heats up the cool air. As the air gets warmer, it lifts up into the sky.

The air already high up in the sky is cold. Can you guess what happens when the rising warm air bumps into the cold air in the sky? The weather changes!

Warm air goes up. Think of a hot-air balloon. A flame heats the air inside the balloon, and the balloon floats into the sky. The balloon stays up as long as the air inside it stays warm.

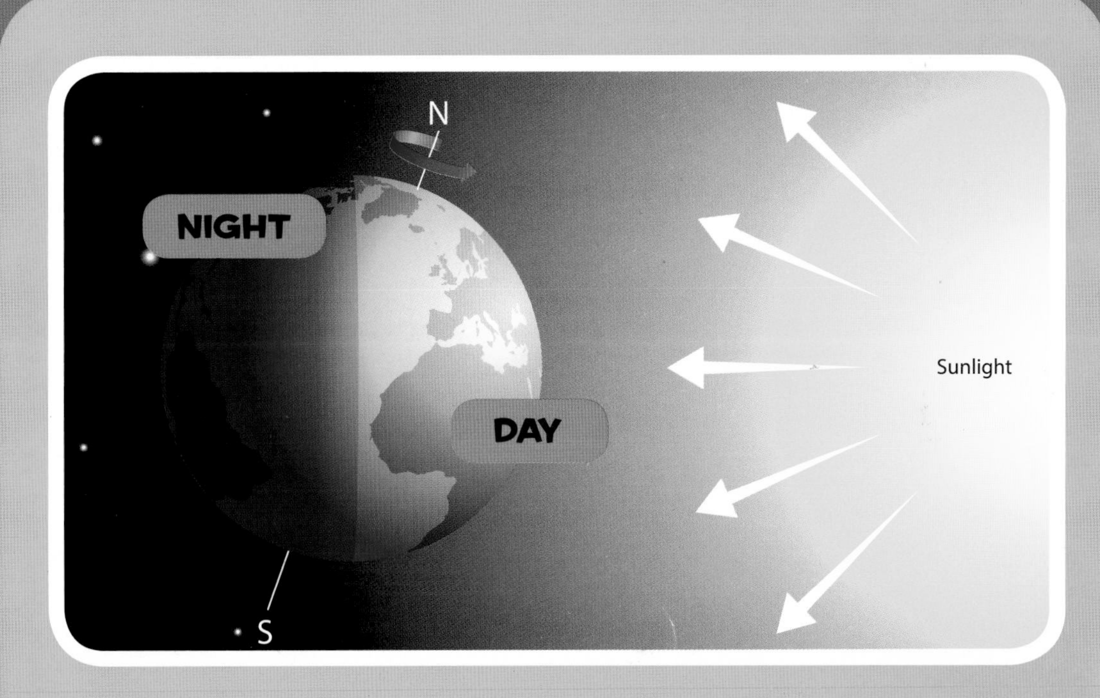

The sun shines all the time. Earth spins around, making day and night. It is daytime on the part of Earth that is facing the sun. It is nighttime on the part facing away.

It is usually **COOLER** in the **MORNING** than in the **AFTERNOON.**

When the sun sets, the sky becomes dark. With no warm sunlight, the ground and air both cool down.

Colder air up in the sky falls to Earth. It pushes away warmer air near the ground. What happens when cold air drives away warm air? The weather changes!

The air feels warmer in the bright sunshine and cooler in the darker shade.

A thermometer **MEASURES THE AIR** temperature.

The **TEMPERATURE** tells if the air is **WARM** or **COLD.**

CHANGING SEASONS

You might live where the weather is always warm. Other places on Earth are always cold. Then there are places where the weather is warm in the summer and cold in the winter. It all depends on how much sunlight shines on that part of the planet. More sunlight means warmer weather.

SPRING

FALL

WINTER

SUMMER

The sun shines all year long, but the weather gets colder or warmer at different times of year. The changes are called seasons. There are four seasons: spring, summer, autumn, and winter.

What are your favorite things to do outside in each season?

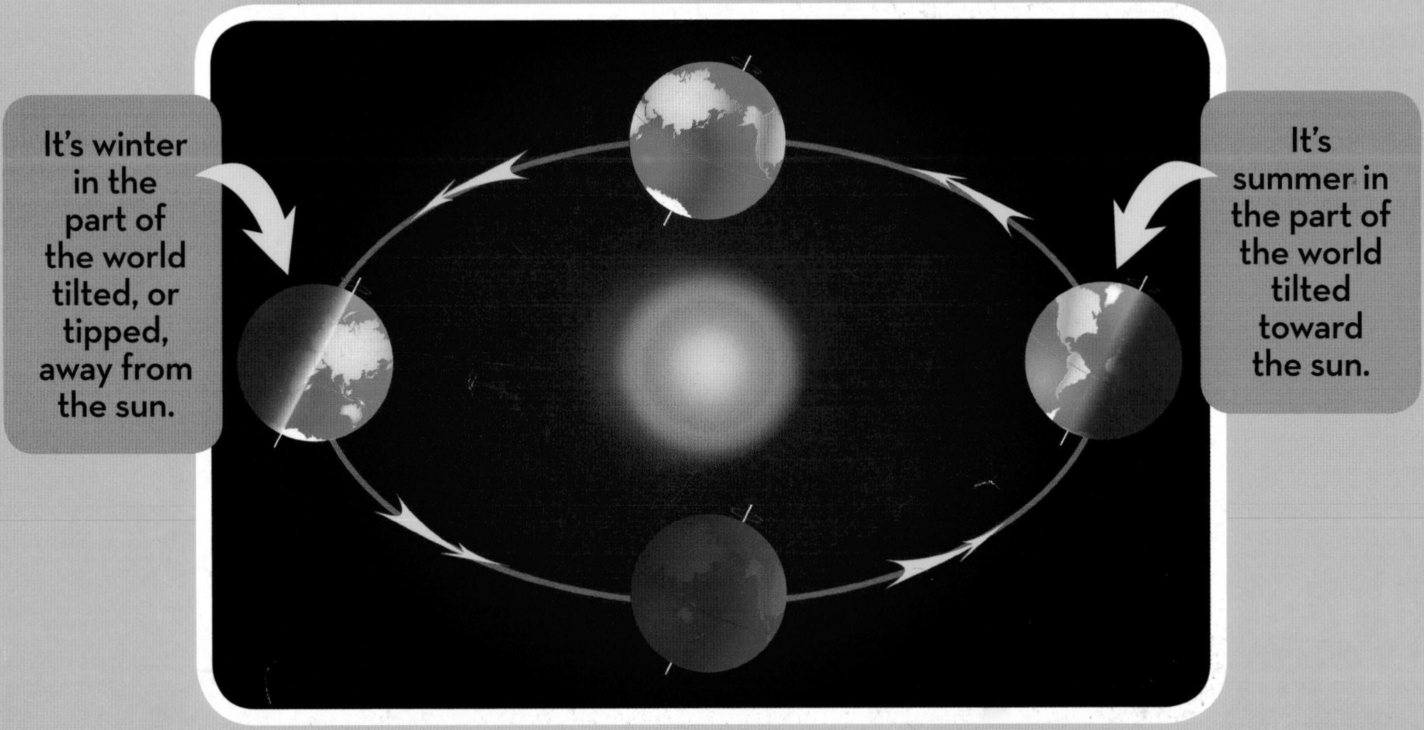

The **EQUATOR** is an imaginary line around the **EARTH.** It divides the planet into a **NORTHERN** half and a **SOUTHERN** half.

It's winter in the part of the world tilted, or tipped, away from the sun.

It's summer in the part of the world tilted toward the sun.

The seasons change because the planet tilts toward or away from the sun.

ANTARCTICA is the **COLDEST** place on **EARTH.**

The places on Earth that get just a little sunlight tend to be cold all the time. It might warm up a little, but there can be snow and ice all year long. The places that get a lot of sunlight are very hot and dry.

Would you rather go on vacation in a cold place or a warm place?

HOT OR COLD?

Look at these pictures. Can you tell which is in a hot place and which is in a cold place?

Earth is 93 million miles (150 million km) away from the sun.

SUN

EARTH

JUST RIGHT FOR LIFE

Even though it gets cold or hot outside, the temperature on Earth is just right for people, plants, and animals to live. Earth is exactly the right distance from the sun. Some people call it a "Goldilocks planet" because it is just the right temperature—just like the last porridge Goldilocks eats in the story "Goldilocks and the Three Bears."

Earth would be too frozen for life if it were farther away from the sun.

Earth would be too hot and dry for things to grow if it were any closer to the sun.

If you live in the mountains, there may be snow in the springtime.

WEATHER WHERE YOU LIVE

If you live near the ocean, it may be windy most of the time.

If you live in a very flat area, a tornado might blow through sometimes.

If you live near a desert, it may be hot during the day.

What sort of weather happens where you live?

ENJOYING THE WEATHER

Some people like it hot. Some like it cold. When it comes to enjoying the outdoors, there's always something for everyone to enjoy.

Hurray! It's snowing! It's fun to get outside to build a snowman or go sledding.

A hot summer day is great weather for playing at the beach.

It is fun to stomp in puddles during a gentle rain without thunder and lightning!

Jumping into leaf piles is perfect fun on a cool autumn day.

What do you like to do in different kinds of weather?

FUN OUTSIDE

Match the activities on the left to the weather on the right.

WEATHER WISE

You might want to check the weather before you step outside. That way, you can plan what to wear and bring along. It is important to be prepared for all types of weather.

An umbrella helps keep you dry on a rainy day. But if the sun is shining, you probably put on sunscreen and sunglasses.

It's good to bundle up to stay warm and dry on a cold winter day.

UMBRELLAS also give you on-the-go SHADE on a sunny, hot day.

Even in winter, **SUNGLASSES** and **SUNSCREEN** protect your face from **BRIGHT SUNLIGHT.**

LET'S PLAY A GAME!

Look at the winter scene and the summer scene. How many things can you find in each scene that do not match the season?

SUMMER

CHAPTER 2
IT'S HOT OUTSIDE

The sun heats up the Earth. Sunlight helps trees and plants grow and makes the temperature rise. Sometimes it can get too hot. Let's learn about hot weather!

FEEL THE HEAT

On a hot, sunny day, sunlight warms up whatever it shines on. That could be you, a tree, a fence, or a building. Pretty soon, all of those warm objects and the ground give off some of the heat they soaked up. That heat warms up the air.

It takes time for the heat from the ground to warm up the air. That's why it's cooler in the morning as the sun is rising. The air is usually warmer in the afternoon.

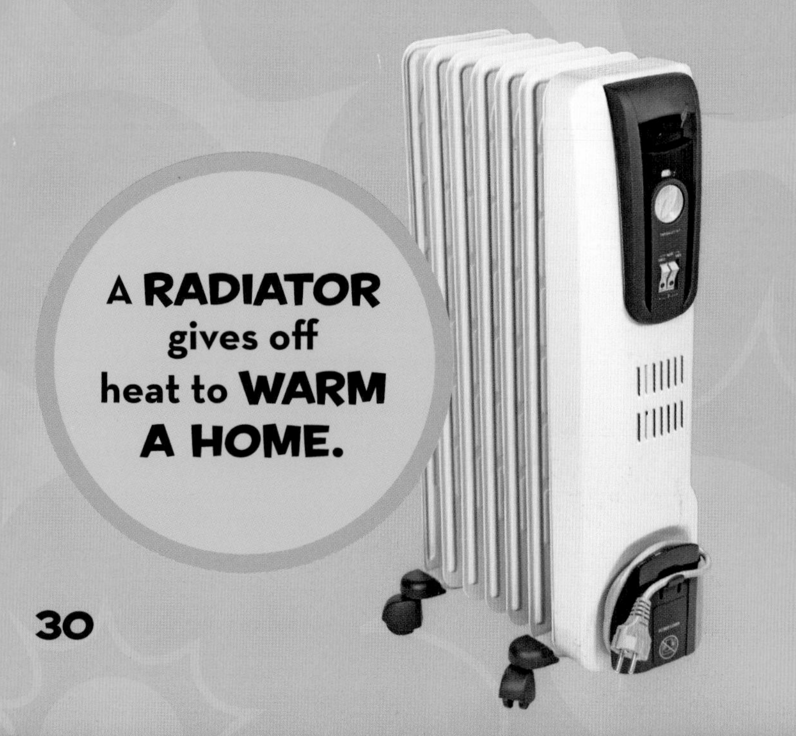

A **RADIATOR** gives off heat to **WARM A HOME.**

After the sun sets, the ground is still warm. Here's why: Without sunlight, the ground slowly gives off heat until it is cool. Think of an oven. If it is opened when it is on, you can feel hot air. After the oven is turned off, it slowly cools down.

Ouch! Sand and sidewalks can be very hot if they have been soaking up hot sunlight for a long time. Better wear sandals!

Water **SOAKS UP HEAT** from the sun. A shaded **SWIMMING POOL** is probably **CHILLY.**

DEATH VALLEY, California, U.S.A., is the **HOTTEST PLACE ON EARTH.** Think of the hottest day you can remember, and then imagine it getting a lot hotter! That will give you **AN IDEA** of how hot Death Valley can be.

IT'S A SCORCHER!

Sunlight helps plants grow and keeps animals warm. But sometimes the sun can make the air temperature get too hot.

Without rain, very hot weather can dry up rivers and farmland. The ground gets so dry that it cracks. People who live in very hot, dry places have to save water.

IT'S HOT OUTSIDE

In some places, the temperature gets so hot that the roads start to melt.

A **HEAT WAVE** is a few days in a row of **VERY HOT AND DRY** weather.

Hot weather with no rain can dry out trees and plants in a forest. A dry forest might catch fire from a bolt of lightning or a campfire that gets out of control.

HOW TO BEAT THE HEAT

Phew, it's hot! Too much running around in the sun can make your body get too hot. That can make you sick with heat exhaustion. It's a good idea to take lots of breaks and drink lots of water in hot weather.

On a really hot day, would you rather drink ice-cold lemonade or steaming hot chocolate?

Too much sunlight can give you a sunburn. It's a good idea to protect your skin.

A sun hat or umbrella give you shade. Sunglasses protect your eyes from bright sunlight.

Sweating helps your body release heat to cool down. Horses and some other animals also sweat.

To keep animals cool, make sure that outdoor pets have some shade, and always keep their water bowls filled.

Dogs don't sweat. They stick out their tongues and pant to shed extra heat.

LET'S PLAY A GAME!

What in the world are these hot-weather things?

Answers: 1. beach umbrella, 2. sand shovel and rake, 3. sunglasses, 4. beach towels, 5. ice-cream cone, 6. ice, 7. swim tube, 8. fan, 9. sprinkler, 10. pool, 11. sand castle, 12. sun hat

CHAPTER 3

WINDY WEATHER

You can feel wind against your skin. You can hear it moving through the trees. You can see it pushing the clouds above. Wind is air on the move.

Wind **MOVES CLOUDS** across the **SKY.**

BLOWING AROUND

Hold on to your hat on a windy day! You can't see the wind, but you can feel it. A gentle breeze tickles your nose.

A strong wind can be fun, but it can also be fierce. Wind pushes sailboats. It also keeps kites flying in the sky.

Wind makes a cold day feel even colder. That feeling is called "wind chill."

WHAT MAKES THE WIND?

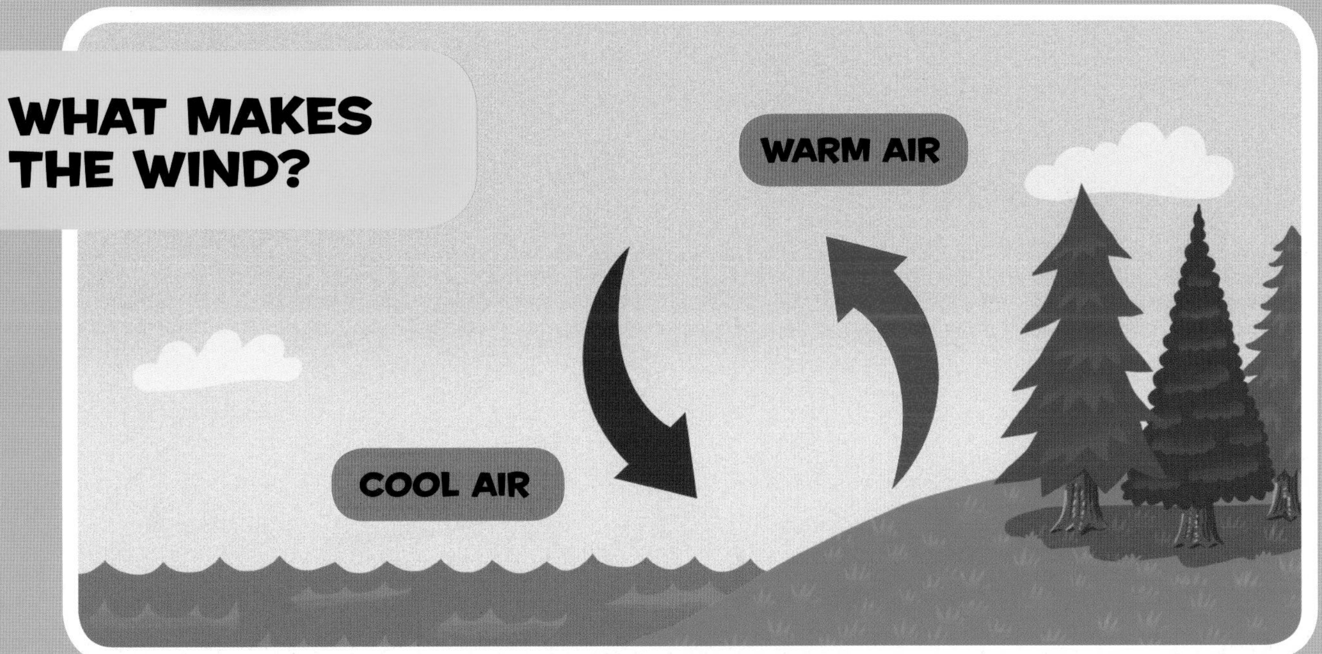

Wind is air that moves around. Air moves when it heats up or cools down. Each morning, the rising sun warms the ground. Heat from the ground warms the air near its surface. Up goes the warm air. High in the sky, the air cools down and sinks to the ground. When it happens over and over, the air starts to move in a circle. That's when the wind blows!

BLOWING THAT-A-WAY

Maybe you have seen leaves blowing in a circle. Wind that swirls around and around is called an eddy.

Wind can blow in any direction—up, down, left, and right. It can even blow around in circles!

Wind can change direction when it bounces off of buildings or hillsides.

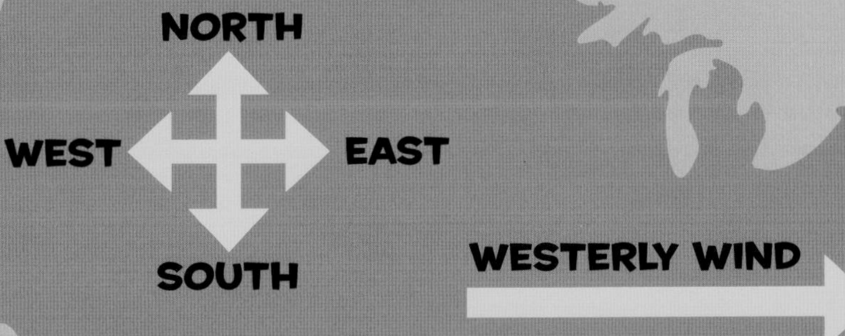

Weather reporters describe wind direction by where it comes from: north, south, east, or west. A westerly wind blows from west to east.

Flying a kite is tricky if the wind keeps changing direction. The kite flips and flops instead of staying up.

WINDS AROUND THE WORLD

Air is always moving around the world. That means the wind is always moving around the world, too. These global winds blow in the same direction along sections of Earth.

Global winds happen for two reasons. First, the sun heats up sections of the planet, and that heats up the air. Then, as the warm air rises, the Earth spins beneath it. The spinning makes the wind curve around the planet.

The **TRADE WINDS** were named long ago when they **PUSHED** big sailing ships across the ocean. The **EXPLORERS** sailing the ships were **DISCOVERING ROUTES** for shipping items to **TRADE** with people around the world.

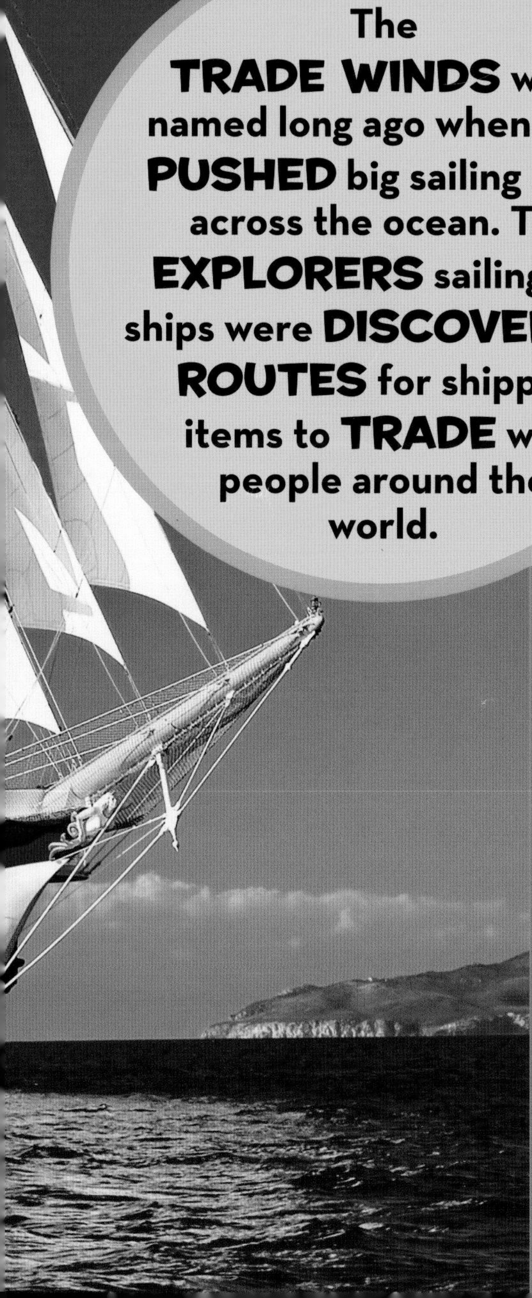

GLOBAL WIND DIRECTIONS

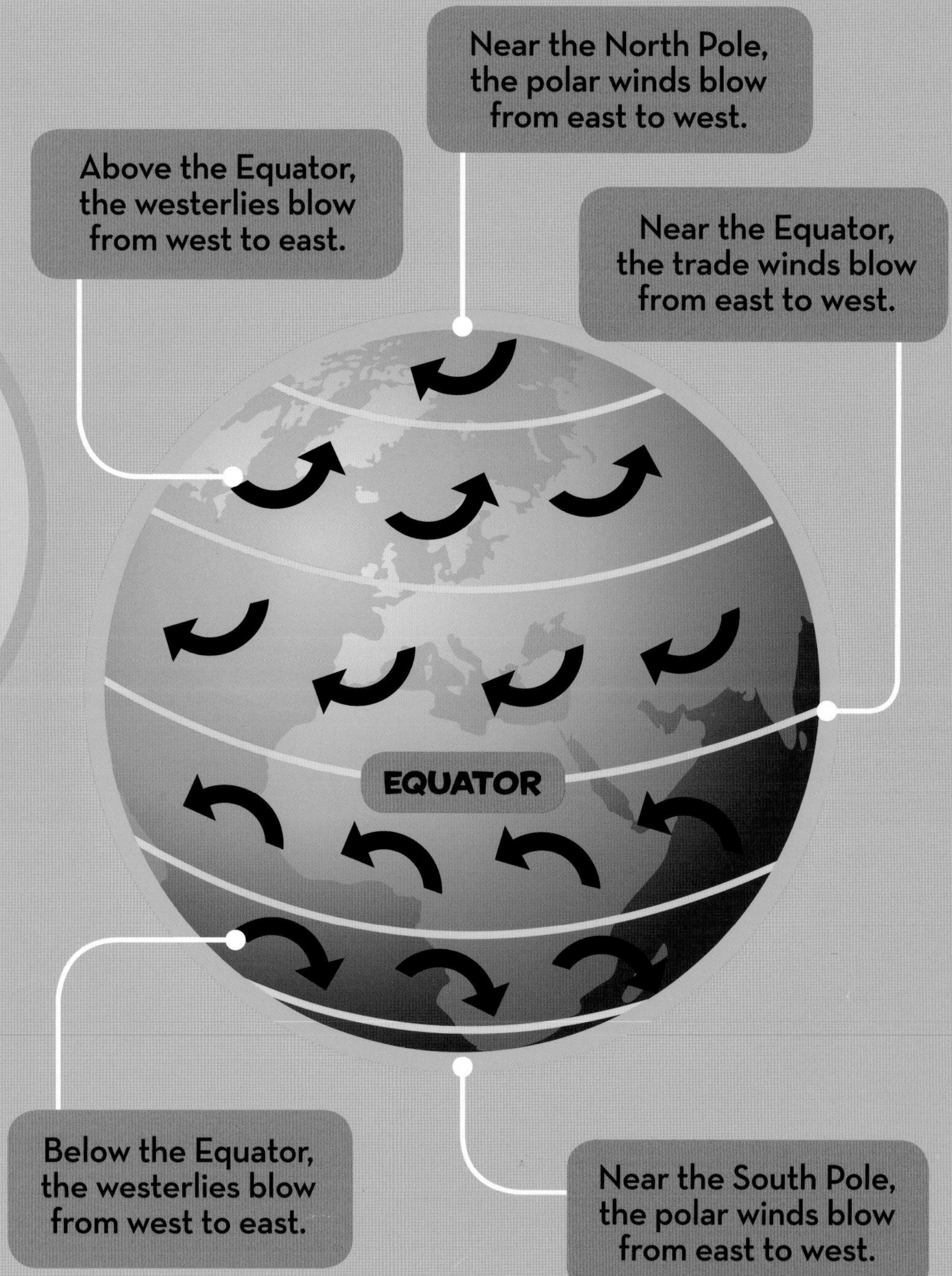

Near the North Pole, the polar winds blow from east to west.

Above the Equator, the westerlies blow from west to east.

Near the Equator, the trade winds blow from east to west.

EQUATOR

Below the Equator, the westerlies blow from west to east.

Near the South Pole, the polar winds blow from east to west.

SPEEDY WIND

Wind can travel at different speeds. If you have used a fan, you have felt the different speeds. The low setting is like a gentle breeze that is not very strong. The high fan setting blows much stronger. In nature, a very fast wind is a very strong wind.

Have you ever chased after a piece of paper blown away by the wind?

"RUN LIKE THE WIND" is a way to say **"RUN AS FAST AS YOU CAN."**

An anemometer (an-uh-MOM-uh-tur) measures wind speed.

On April 12, 1934, a weather station on top of Mount Washington in New Hampshire, U.S.A., recorded the wind blowing at 231 miles an hour (372 km/h). That's as fast as a race car.

BEAUFORT SCALE

More than 200 years ago, a sailor named Francis Beaufort created a chart for wind speed. The Beaufort scale is still used today.

WIND FORCE

- **0** no wind
- **1** light air barely felt on the face
- **2** light breeze that can blow dust
- **3** gentle breeze that can move leaves
- **4** mild breeze that moves branches
- **5** steady breeze that makes small trees sway
- **6** strong breeze that moves large branches
- **7** wind that pushes against you
- **8** strong wind that makes it hard to walk
- **9** very strong wind that blows down tents
- **10** storm wind that blows down trees
- **11** violent storm that damages houses
- **12** hurricane wind that destroys houses

CHICAGO, ILLINOIS, U.S.A.

WINDY PLACES

A **SEA BREEZE** is air moving from the **WATER TO THE LAND.**

In some places, the wind blows a lot. The U.S. city of Chicago is a windy place. A lot of Chicago's wind comes from the air above nearby Lake Michigan. The sun heats up the land faster than it heats up the water in the lake. When the air in the city rises, the cooler air over the lake moves toward the land. This air movement makes a lot of wind.

ANTARCTICA

Antarctica is the windiest continent on Earth. Cold air rushes downhill from the center of the continent toward the sea in all directions.

Thanks to **OCEAN WINDS** that are **SQUEEZED** between two big islands, **WELLINGTON,** New Zealand, is the **WINDIEST CITY** on Earth.

WELLINGTON, NEW ZEALAND

WINDSTORMS

HABOOB

Close the windows and shut the door! A superstrong wind is headed your way. It is important to get indoors quickly when a windstorm is coming.

In the desert, fast-moving winds can kick up mountains of dust and sand. These storms are called haboobs.

MOUNT EVEREST

Cold air at the top of a mountain flows down snowy slopes. Like a runaway snowboard, the wind gets faster and faster. This cold katabatic (kat-uh-BAT-ick) wind can race downhill faster than 100 miles an hour (161 km/h).

A thunderstorm can push a huge wall of wind in front of it. This invisible wind wall is called a derecho (deh-REH-cho). The wind can blow as fast as 130 miles an hour (209 km/h). That's twice as fast as cars go on the highway.

The word **"DERECHO"** is Spanish for **"STRAIGHT,** not curved."

DERECHO

WIND DID THAT!

Corsica, an island in the Mediterranean Sea, is so windy that trees like this one grow shaped in the direction the wind blows.

Strong winds blowing from Lake Michigan carved these crazy sculptures in the frozen sand at Silver Beach County Park in St. Joseph, Michigan, U.S.A.

Wind can shape and sculpt the landscape. A steady wind can cause erosion—blowing away tiny bits of dirt and rocks over a long period of time.

Sometimes the wind can blow so hard, it rearranges a neighborhood with one giant gust!

During Hurricane Sandy, this tree blew over onto a house in Brooklyn, New York, U.S.A.

STRONG winds have a lot of energy. **WIND TURBINES** turn that energy into electricity.

LET'S PLAY A GAME!

Point to the pictures that show the wind blowing. How can you tell? Can you spot any pictures where no wind is blowing? How do you know?

CHAPTER 4
CLOUDY SKIES

Clouds that block the sun create shade on a hot day. They look like cotton, but they are really bunches of tiny drops of water high in the sky. Sometimes it is hard to tell if the sky is partly cloudy or partly sunny!

CLOUDS ABOVE

Clouds look **SOLID,** but you **COULD WALK** through them.

SOME clouds have **ENOUGH WATER** to make rain.

CLOUDS sometimes have **ICE AND DIRT** in them.

Do you see a whale made of clouds in the sky? Or a dragon? It is fun to pick out shapes in puffy white clouds. Sometimes clouds look like ribbons across the sky. No matter what clouds look like, they are all made of the same thing: water floating in the sky.

Imagine a pot of water on the stove. When it gets hot, the water turns into steam that rises into the air.

Now imagine the ground as a giant pot of water. There are tiny drops of water everywhere. When the sun warms up the ground, the water turns into invisible steam, also called vapor (VAY-pur). Just like steam from a hot pot, the water vapor rises into the air.

STEAM

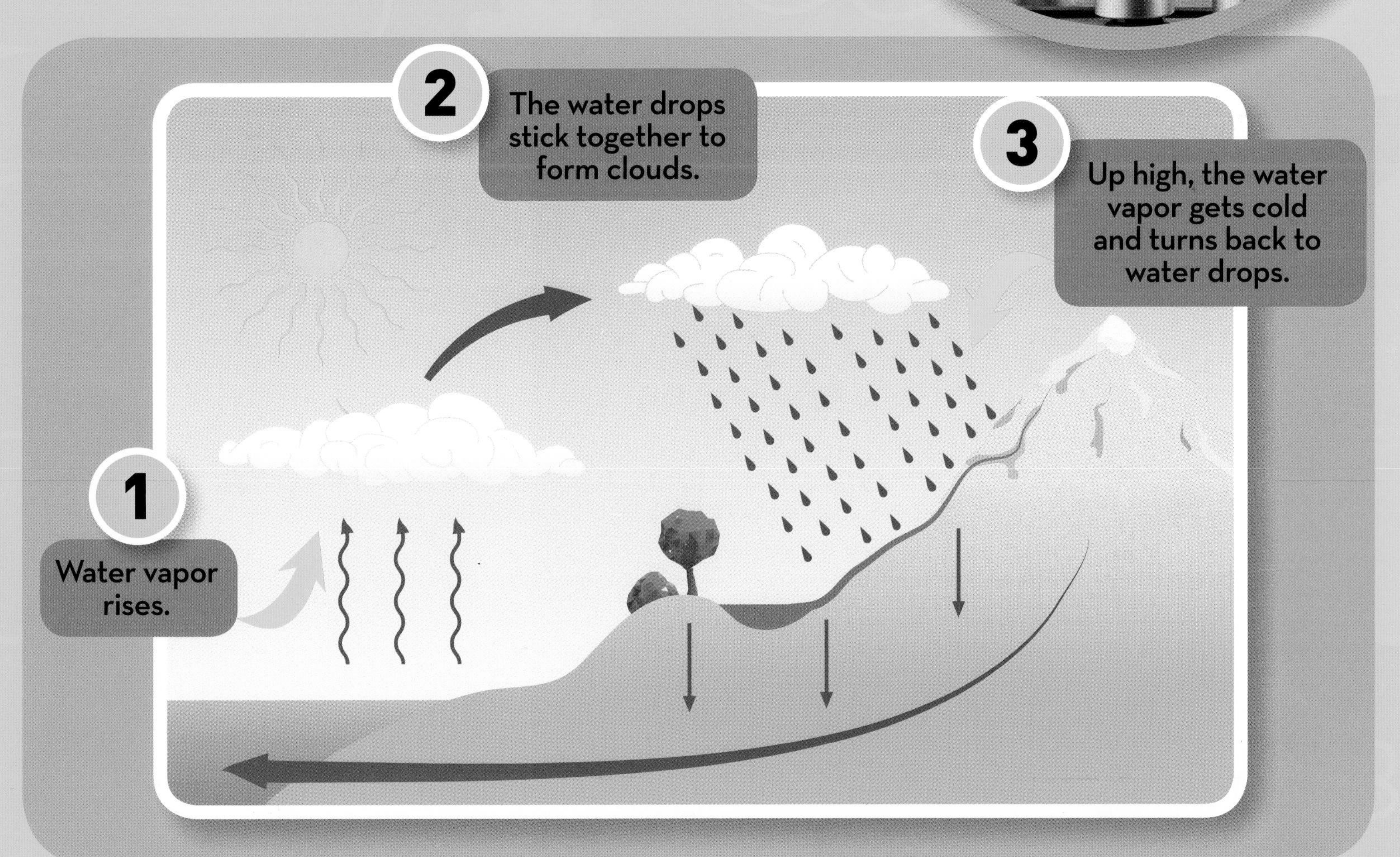

KINDS OF CLOUDS

CUMULUS

STRATUS

Short, tall, puffy, thin—clouds come in all sorts of shapes and sizes.

Big puffy white clouds that look like cotton balls are called cumulus (KYOOM-yuh-lus) clouds.

Gray flat clouds covering the sky are called stratus clouds.

High, thin, feathery clouds are called cirrus (SEER-us) clouds.

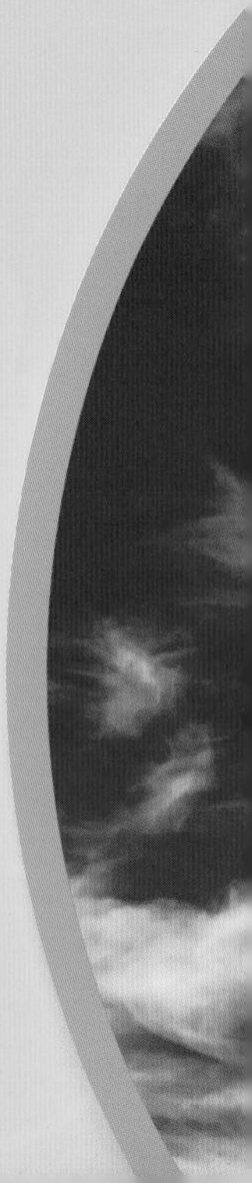

Do you like puffy clouds or thin clouds better?

Some long clouds that stretch across the sky are made by airplanes. These cloud strips are called contrails. They form like clouds very high in the sky because airplanes give off water vapor.

CIRRUS

FOG

Fog can **FEEL COLD** and **DAMP.**

Sometimes in the morning you might think the world looks a little cloudy. It might be hard to see a tree in front of your nose! That's because there is a cloud near the ground. It is also called fog.

Fog happens when there is a lot of water vapor near the ground. It stays cool and forms a cloud there. Fog usually disappears by late morning when sunlight makes the air warmer and it rises into the sky.

Sometimes tall buildings **TOWER ABOVE** low-lying fog.

Fog can be so thick that you can't see through it. Driving in thick fog is dangerous.

Sailors rely on the light from lighthouses to help them find their way in the fog.

Does your bathroom fog up when you take a hot bath or shower?

LIGHTHOUSE IN CAPE ELIZABETH, MAINE, U.S.A.

LET'S PLAY A GAME!

Look at these pictures of clouds. What shapes do you see in them? Draw what you see. Now turn the book upside down. Do you see different shapes?

CHAPTER 5
WHEN IT RAINS

As raindrops fall from clouds, they bring water back down to Earth. Rain is an important part of nature. Without it, many plants would not grow.

DRIP DROP, DRIP DROP

It's raining outside. One by one, drops of water fall from the sky. Rain moves water from the clouds down to the ground. Without rain, the ground will dry up.

It's fun to run around in a warm, gentle summer rain shower!

RAINDROPS make different **SOUNDS** depending on **WHERE** they land.

Umbrellas **GO UP** when rain **COMES DOWN!**

What is your favorite way to enjoy the rain?

A **RAIN BARREL** collects rain to save for use during **DRY WEATHER.**

A **LIGHT RAIN** is also called a **DRIZZLE.**

Rainbows are stripes of color in the sky. A rainbow happens when sunlight shines through tiny raindrops floating in the air.

Look for a **RAINBOW** the next time **THE SUN COMES OUT** after a rain shower ends.

A person in an airplane can see a rainbow as a circle. A person on the ground sees only the top half of the circle. That's because the ground blocks the view of the bottom half.

Rain starts as tiny drops of water in a cloud. The water drops bump into each other and stick together. They grow bigger and bigger. Soon the big water drops are so heavy that they fall from the cloud. It's raining!

There is a saying, "APRIL SHOWERS BRING MAY FLOWERS." Rain showers help flowers grow.

When it **RAINS**, weather reporters on TV say, **"IT IS WET OUTSIDE TODAY."**

Raindrops change size and shape as they fall. They start as tiny circles. They stick to other raindrops in the sky and get bigger. Big raindrops look like beans when they fall. If they get too big, they break apart into tiny circles again.

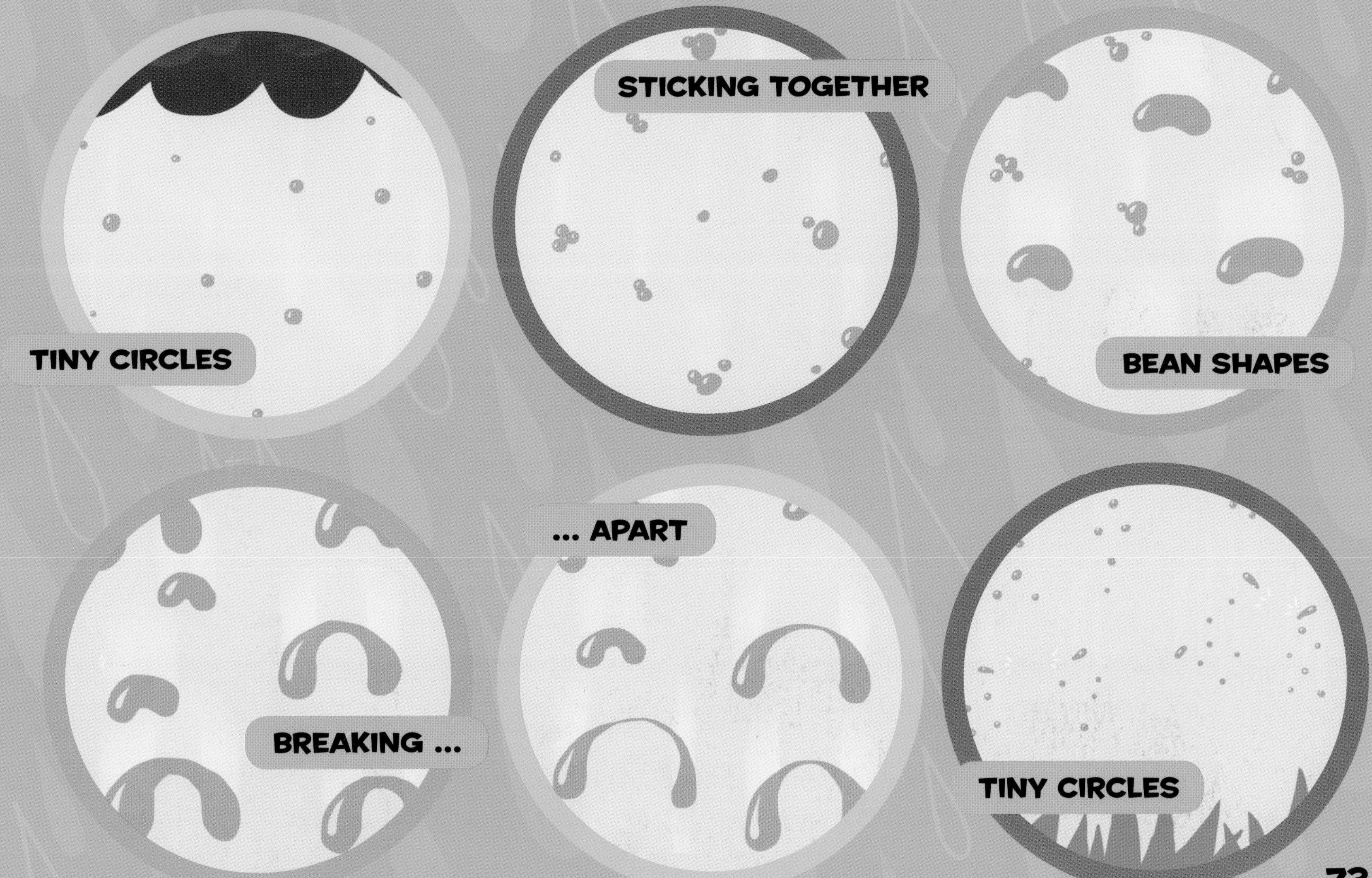

TINY CIRCLES

STICKING TOGETHER

BEAN SHAPES

BREAKING ...

... APART

TINY CIRCLES

RAIN, RAIN, RAIN

It rains nearly every day in some places. In other places, it almost never rains. The amount of rain depends on how much water vapor is in the air.

Death Valley is a desert in California, U.S.A. It gets only about two inches (5 cm) of rain each year.

In one year, the top of Mount Waialeale (wie-AH-lay-AH-lay) in Hawaii, U.S.A., gets about 35 feet (10.7 m) of rain.

Death Valley, California

The **GROUND** soaks up **WATER THAT FALLS** when it rains.

PLANTS and **ANIMALS** need water to **LIVE.**

African elephants in Kenya, Africa

In some parts of the world, it rains mostly during the rainy season. In southern Africa, the rainy season is from October to April.

Subtropical forest in Nepal

It is wet and rainy most of the time in a tropical rain forest. There are lots of trees and plants because there is plenty of water to go around.

TOO MUCH RAIN

Destruction from a mudslide

When there is too much rain, the ground gets so wet that it can't soak up any more water. That's when danger can strike. It is important to listen to weather reports and steer clear of high water and muddy ground.

Watch out! Mudslide! Hillsides get soggy and muddy when it rains a lot. The ground can slide away in a mudslide. Mudslides are very dangerous.

WHEN IT RAINS

Too much rain can make rivers overflow. The water can flood villages and cities. In some places, houses are built on stilts to stay above high water.

Some families in the country of Bangladesh use floating gardens so they can grow food even in a flood.

A garden can **FLOAT** on a raft made out of **BAMBOO** and weeds called **WATER HYACINTH.**

FLOATING GARDEN

THUNDERSTORMS

Tall, dark clouds roll in. They block the sun and push a fierce wind along the ground. *Crack!* Lightning flashes from the cloud as thunder booms across the sky. It's a thunderstorm!

Lightning happens when electricity builds up inside a thundercloud. Have you ever walked across a rug in your socks? You are building up static electricity. If you touch something, you might feel a mini zap. Lightning is a really big zap.

AROUND THE WORLD, lightning flashes 100 times **EACH SECOND.**

Lightning can strike trees, houses, cars, and even people. Don't stand under a tree or go swimming during a thunderstorm. The safest place is inside a building.

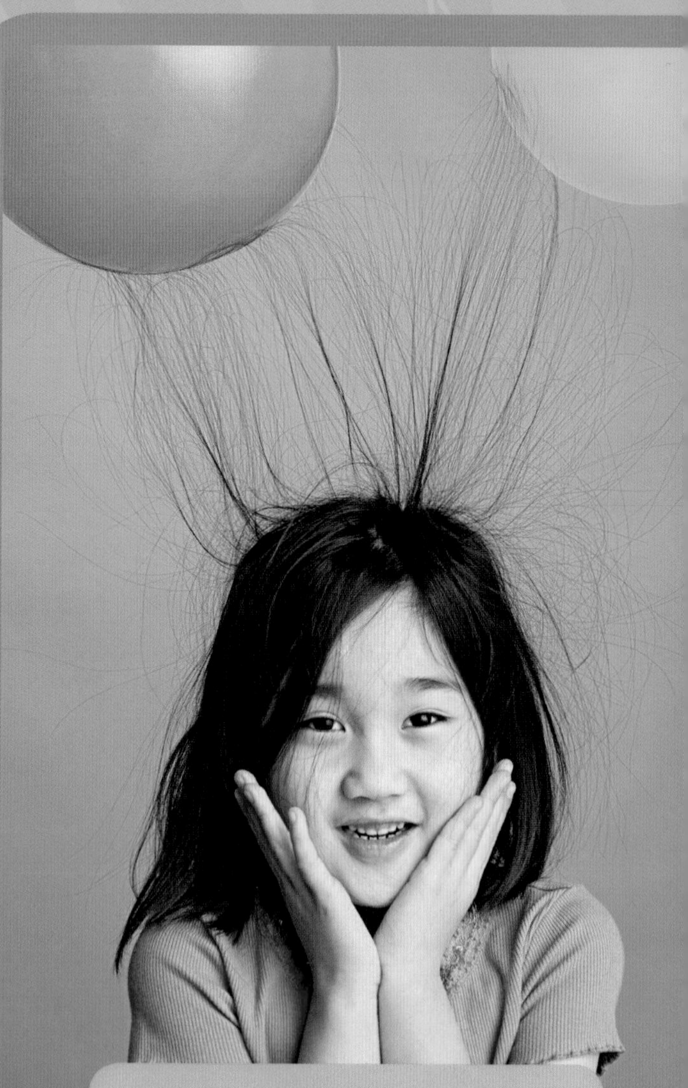

Rubbing balloons against your head creates static electricity.

Sprites are bursts of electricity high above a thundercloud. Sprites look like jellyfish.

A lightning rod protects a house from a bolt of lightning. The lightning hits the rod instead of the house. Electricity travels down a wire into the ground. The house is safe.

LIGHTNING ROD

THUNDER always comes after **LIGHTNING.**

Thunder is a loud clap of air. The lightning quickly moves air apart. The air booms when it slaps back together. It's like when you clap your hands but a lot louder!

Ice balls called hail can drop from a thundercloud during a big storm. They are frozen raindrops that grow big inside a very tall cloud.

REALLY BIG STORMS

Strong winds circle over the ocean. The clouds begin to spin. Rain hammers the water surface. A hurricane is forming!

Hurricanes usually form over a part of the ocean where the air and water are warm. Trouble happens when the storm moves toward land.

A hurricane can cause flooding and knock down trees. It can also cause huge waves that knock down seaside buildings.

The wind speed of a hurricane can be as fast as a high-speed train!

Hurricanes are also called CYCLONES and TYPHOONS.

Hurricane Isabel, 2003

Hurricanes usually form NEAR the EQUATOR.

HURRICANE NAMES

Hurricanes and tropical storms coming from the Atlantic Ocean are named so people can easily find out information about them. Each year, the World Meteorological Organization names the storms in alphabetical order according to a list for that year. The names are repeated every six years.

2015	2016	2017	2018	2019	2020
Ana	Alex	Arlene	Alberto	Andrea	Arthur
Bill	Bonnie	Bret	Beryl	Barry	Bertha
Claudette	Colin	Cindy	Chris	Chantal	Cristobal
Danny	Danielle	Don	Debby	Dorian	Dolly
Erika	Earl	Emily	Ernesto	Erin	Edouard
Fred	Fiona	Franklin	Florence	Fernand	Fay
Grace	Gaston	Gert	Gordon	Gabrielle	Gonzalo
Henri	Hermine	Harvey	Helene	Humberto	Hanna
Ida	Ian	Irma	Isaac	Imelda	Isaias
Joaquin	Julia	Jose	Joyce	Jerry	Josephine
Kate	Karl	Katia	Kirk	Karen	Kyle
Larry	Lisa	Lee	Leslie	Lorenzo	Laura
Mindy	Matthew	Maria	Michael	Melissa	Marco
Nicholas	Nicole	Nate	Nadine	Nestor	Nana
Odette	Otto	Ophelia	Oscar	Olga	Omar
Peter	Paula	Philippe	Patty	Pablo	Paulette
Rose	Richard	Rina	Rafael	Rebekah	Rene
Sam	Shary	Sean	Sara	Sebastien	Sally
Teresa	Tobias	Tammy	Tony	Tanya	Teddy
Victor	Virginie	Vince	Valerie	Van	Vicky
Wanda	Walter	Whitney	William	Wendy	Wilfred

Sometimes a thunderstorm sprouts a spinning cloud that touches the ground. Stay away! That is the dangerous funnel of a tornado. A tornado forms when strong winds spin inside very tall thunderclouds.

The wind in and around a tornado is very strong. It can pick up people, animals, buses, and even houses off the ground.

Tornado in Australia

SPINNING tornadoes are also called TWISTERS.

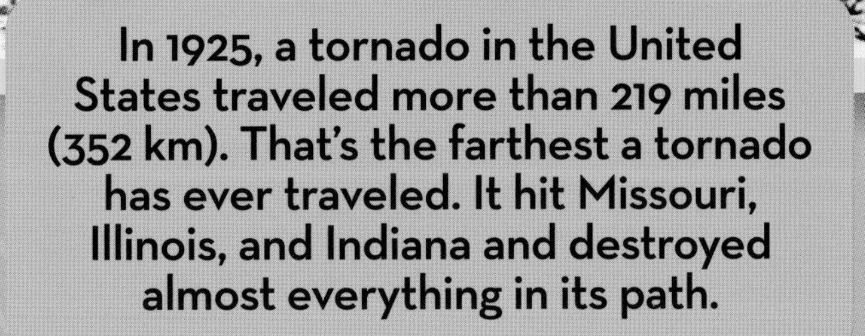

In 1925, a tornado in the United States traveled more than 219 miles (352 km). That's the farthest a tornado has ever traveled. It hit Missouri, Illinois, and Indiana and destroyed almost everything in its path.

DOROTHY'S house **FLEW** in a tornado in ***THE WIZARD OF OZ.***

Tornado in Colorado, U.S.A.

BE SAFE!

- Safety is key if a tornado is on its way.
- Your parents will listen to weather reports and local safety authorities for information.
- Sometimes people are asked to leave the area. If not, they should be sure to get indoors.
- If you hear a thunder rumble that doesn't stop, get indoors. Hide in a basement or a room with no windows.
- You can also stay safe by lying down in a bathtub.
- If you are outside, lie down in a ditch away from buildings, trees, and cars.

Storm chasers **HELP** keep people **SAFE** by **WARNING** them about big storms.

STORM CHASERS

A big storm is brewing! Some people, called "storm chasers," watch for the worst weather possible. Storm chasers try to get close to storms. They want to find out as much as they can about the storms.

Storm chasers don't follow just any storm. It has to be a big weather event that is dangerous and might damage property. Sometimes the storm chases the storm chasers.

You need to know a lot about weather to be a storm chaser. Professional weather scientists are called meteorologists (mee-tee-uh-ROL-uh-gists), and many of them are also storm chasers.

Storm chasers use computers to help them find out what kind of storm they are following. They also need to know which direction the storm is heading.

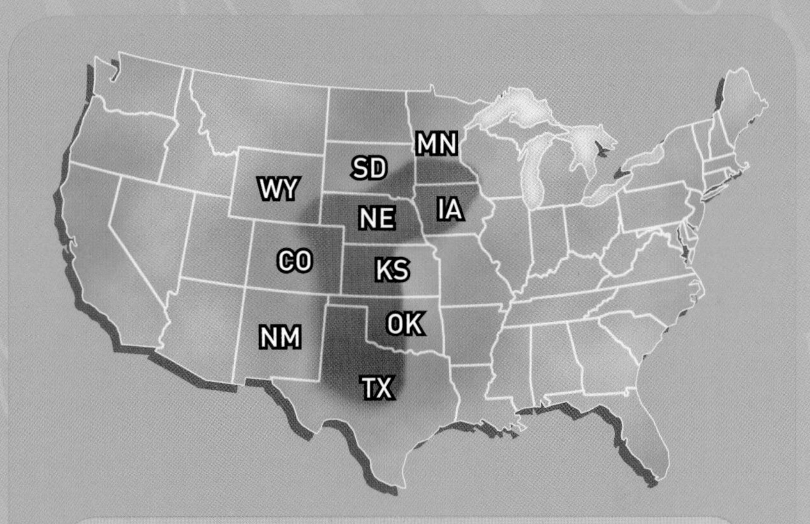

The middle of the United States is called Tornado Alley because more tornadoes happen there than anywhere else.

If you were a storm chaser, what would you invent to help you study storms?

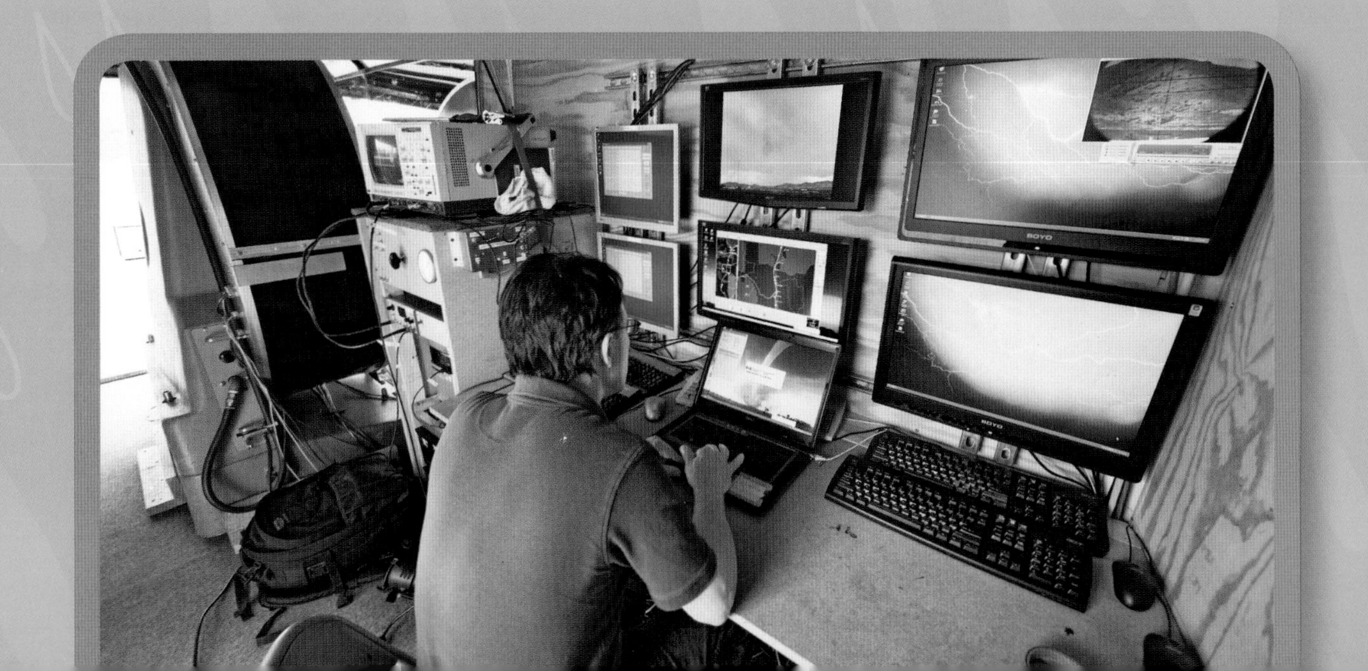

A storm is forming … let's get going! Armored trucks help keep storm chasers safe while they gather details about the storm.

Cameras take video of the storm.

Thick plastic safety windows protect the storm chasers inside.

Armored plates protect against flying trees and pieces of buildings.

Side panels block wind to keep it from flipping the truck.

Radar, antennae, and other sensors collect information about the storm.

Sensors called **TURTLES** get **SWEPT UP** by a storm to **COLLECT INFORMATION** from inside.

Sometimes storm chasers fly airplanes into bad weather … on purpose! They gather details about a storm using sensors that measure the temperature, wind speed, and other details. The plane drops the sensors into the storm. The sensors send information back to the storm chasers.

LET'S PLAY A GAME!

Can you match the picture to the words that describe the type of weather shown?

Answers: 1. hurricane, 2. tornado, 3. partly sunny, 4. thunderstorm, 5. rainy

CHAPTER 6
BRRR! IT'S COLD

It's winter! Playing in the snow is so much fun. Icicles, snowflakes, and snow crunching under your boots are just some of the great things about cold weather. There's so much more!

A CHILL IN THE AIR

How many words can you think of that describe cold weather?

When the weather turns chilly, it is time to close the windows to keep the house warm. You might want to find your coat, hat, and mittens, too. It's winter!

How cold is it outside? A thermometer measures the temperature.

At the end of a hot summer, 50°F (10°C) might seem cold to you. At the end of a cold winter, 50°F might seem warm to you.

Your breath looks like a cloud when the air is cold. That's because your breath comes out as warm water vapor.

Dogs called huskies have thick coats to keep them warm in winter. Some dogs have almost no fur, so they need jackets to stay warm.

Cold weather means rest time for many plants and animals. Plants stop growing to survive in the cold.

A lot of animals also rest in winter. Bears hunker down in dens and go into a deep sleep. This is called hibernation.

Not every animal sleeps through the cold winter. Horses like to kick up their heels and play when the weather gets nippy.

JACK FROST is a nickname for **COLD WEATHER** that **STINGS YOUR NOSE.**

HUSKY

Black bear hibernating

It feels **COLDER** when the wind blows. That **WIND CHILL,** or "feels like" temperature, can make it feel like **10°F (-12°C)** even if the thermometer reads **20°F (-7°C).**

FROZEN!

Icicles, ice pops, ice cubes, and ice palaces are all fun to enjoy. Ice is frozen water.

If you put liquid water into a freezer, it becomes so cold that it turns into solid ice. Water freezes outdoors when the air temperature drops below 32°F (0°C).

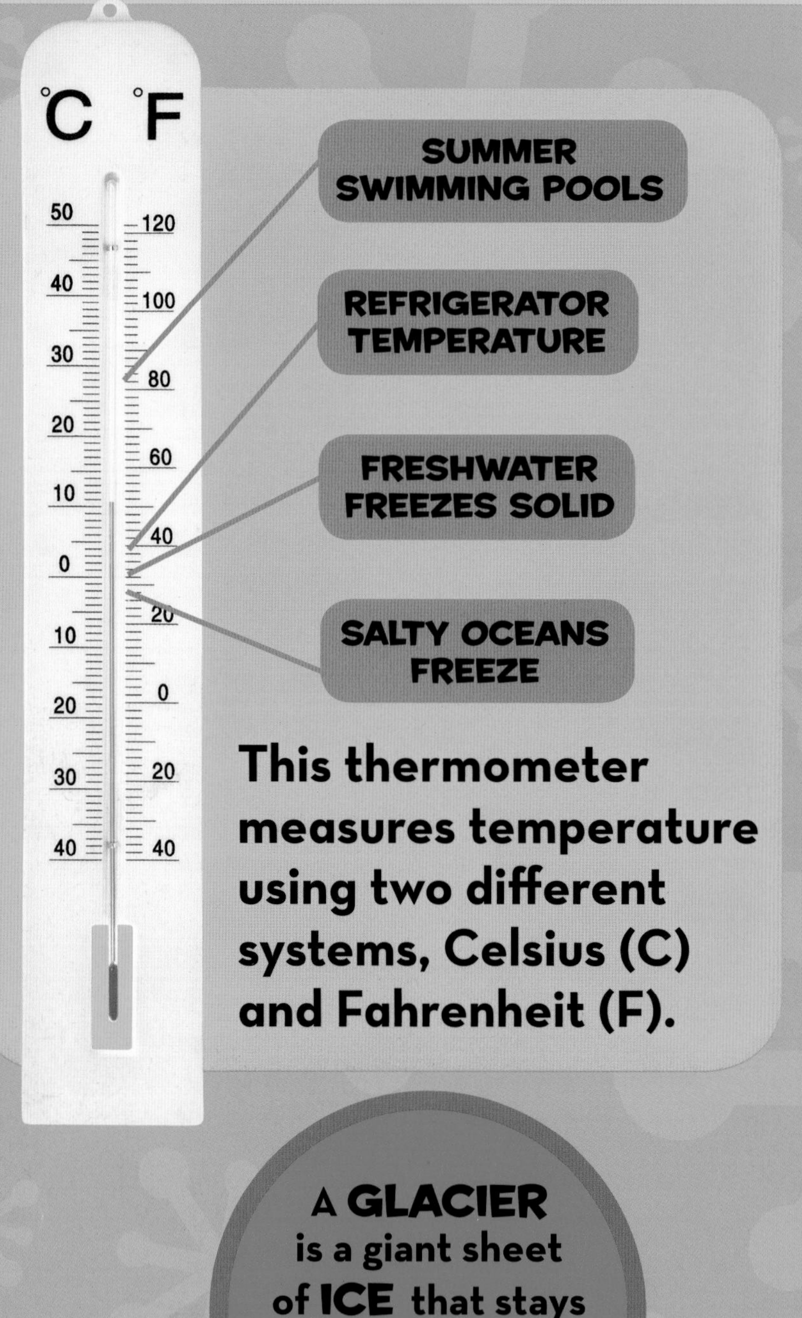

This thermometer measures temperature using two different systems, Celsius (C) and Fahrenheit (F).

A GLACIER is a giant sheet of ICE that stays frozen ALL YEAR LONG.

People in Harbin City, China, enjoy visiting this building made of ice at an annual festival.

Water is made of little packets of chemicals called molecules. They move all around in the liquid. When the water gets cold, the molecules slow down and start to stick together. Solid ice forms when all of the molecules stick together in a neat pattern called a crystal.

Where have you seen ice in the kitchen?

Lakes and streams might not freeze right away if the air is below 32°F. The water takes some time to get cold. Ice forms on the surface and slowly gets thicker.

Deep lakes stay unfrozen far below the surface. The deep water is cold, but plants and animals can still live in it.

Ice can be strong as long as it is thick enough. Ice should be at least four inches (10 cm) thick to hold a person. That is what eight copies of this book stacked on top of each other measures.

WARNING: Never walk out onto a frozen body of water unless you are with a trusted adult in an area designated for ice skating or such activities.

LET IT SNOW!

A **BLIZZARD** is a heavy snowstorm with **STRONG WIND.**

You can have lots of adventures and fun playing in snow. You can build a snowman. Maybe you like to go sledding. You might build an igloo. Even shoveling snow can be fun!

Some snow is light and fluffy. It is perfect for skiing and snowboarding. Sometimes snow is wet and sticky. This kind of snow is great for building a snowman.

Strong wind can peel away a layer of snow and roll it up.

If you could build anything out of snow, what would it be?

Snowflakes form inside a cloud when water vapor freezes around pieces of dust. Snowflakes come in lots of beautiful shapes. Each snowflake looks different.

A flurry is a light snow. In the movie *Frozen*, Olaf the snowman gets his own personal flurry so he won't melt if the weather isn't cold enough.

OLAF THE SNOWMAN

An **AVALANCHE** happens when snow suddenly **SLIDES** down a **STEEP MOUNTAIN.** Avalanches move very fast and can **BURY WHOLE TOWNS.**

Snowfields **STAY ALL YEAR** on mountaintops where the **AIR IS COLD** all the time.

COLD-WEATHER STORMS

SNOWPLOW

When the outside air is cold enough to freeze water, snow or sleet will fall instead of rain. There are a few different types of winter storms. What kind of storm develops depends on how cold and wet the air is.

A winter storm starts when a warm patch of air bumps into a cold patch. Lighter warm air rises over the heavier cold air. Water vapor in the clouds turns into tiny ice crystals called snowflakes.

Sometimes warm air gets sandwiched between two layers of cold air. This makes different types of winter storms.

FROSTBITE happens when your **SKIN** gets so cold it **FREEZES.** Cover up!

When snow falls through warm air, it melts into **RAINDROPS.**

FREEZING RAIN falls when raindrops get very cold but don't freeze in the air. They freeze as soon as they touch an ice-cold object, such as a mailbox or a street.

SLEET falls when raindrops refreeze into ice before they hit the ground.

SNOW falls when the air stays cold. Snowflakes stay frozen all the way from the clouds to the ground.

ICE STORMS

Whoa! An ice storm covered everything in ice. Buildings, bikes, branches … everything!

An ice storm is a freezing rain that coats surfaces with ice. Supercold raindrops instantly freeze when they hit anything cold.

The movie ***ICE AGE*** takes place during a time when most of the **PLANET** was **COVERED IN ICE.**

SID THE SLOTH

After an **ICE STORM,** sidewalks are slippery. **BRANCHES** can fall from trees. **POWER LINES** can break. It is best to **STAY INDOORS** until things warm up and the **ICE MELTS.**

Bicycle after an ice storm

Cars after an ice storm

What do you think would be the most amazing thing to see covered in ice?

The world looks different after an ice storm. Car doors are frozen shut. Trees are bent over under the heavy ice. Power lines droop to the ground. Just a half inch (1.3 cm) of ice adds hundreds of pounds to a power line between two towers.

WINTER A-WEAR

It snowed! It's time to have some outdoor fun, but it is important to be prepared.

Staying warm is key. That means staying dry with the help of the right clothes and gear. It's best to wear three layers in really cold weather. Be sure to close zippers and wear mittens and boots to keep the snow out.

COTTON clothes get **COLD** if they get **WET.** Clothes made of **WOOL** and **POLYESTER** help keep you **WARMER** than cotton even if they get wet.

What's your favorite thing to do when you play outside in the snow?

An **ARCTIC FOX** stays warm thanks to a **LAYERED FUR COAT** and a **BUSHY TAIL** that it can **CURL** around itself.

LET'S PLAY A GAME!

Help the snowman find his way through the snow to get his hat.

END

CHAPTER 7
KNOWING THE WEATHER

Understanding the weather helps people stay safe when big storms are forming. There are many tools, from wind socks to computers, that experts use to study the weather.

WEATHER TALES

People have always wondered what makes the weather. Long ago, people made up stories to explain the weather. People with superpowers threw spears to make thunder. A magic snake made rainbows. An eagle created wind with its wings.

Over time, scientists began to study the weather to figure out how it works. However, some of the old stories are still around today as fun traditions.

ZEUS was a god in stories told in **ANCIENT GREECE.** He had the power to throw **LIGHTNING BOLTS** at his enemies.

ZEUS

In the United States, February 2 is Groundhog Day. A groundhog named Punxsutawney Phil sneaks out of his burrow. If he sees his shadow, there will be six more weeks of winter. No shadow means winter will end soon … or so the story goes!

PUNXSUTAWNEY PHIL

An ancient Greek scientist named Aristotle was one of the first people to study why weather happens. He wrote a book called *Meteorology*. Today, weather scientists are called meteorologists.

ARISTOTLE

Some people read the *Old Farmer's Almanac* to find out what the weather might be in the next year. This forecast comes from looking at past weather patterns using a secret method known only to those who work on the almanac.

What stories do you know about the weather?

TODAY'S WEATHER

You can hear a weather report on the radio or watch it on TV. A weather report includes a forecast, which describes what weather to expect. Almost everybody wants to know what the weather is going to be like each day or even for the whole week.

It is good to know if a big storm is coming. People can plan to stay at home and out of danger.

It is also good to know if the weather will be sunny for a picnic or a day at the beach.

How do you find out what the weather where you live is going to be each day?

NOBODY can **CONTROL THE WEATHER.** But everyone can **PREPARE** for it.

Daily weather reports help people decide what to wear. It might be chilly now, but the weather report says it will warm up. It sounds like a good idea to wear a jacket in the morning and short sleeves in the afternoon.

Surfers tune in to weather reports to find the best ocean waves. Wind kicks up big waves far away from the shore. Surf's up!

Many birds fly south for warm weather during the winter. The birds can tell that winter is coming because of shorter days, colder temperatures, and less food to eat.

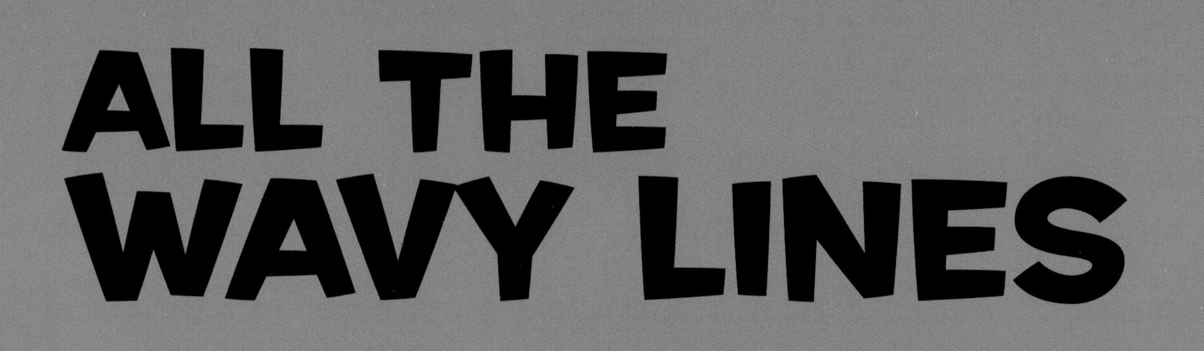

ALL THE WAVY LINES

A weather map has lots of wavy lines with dots, triangles, and arrows. To a meteorologist, these lines and arrows tell the story of the weather.

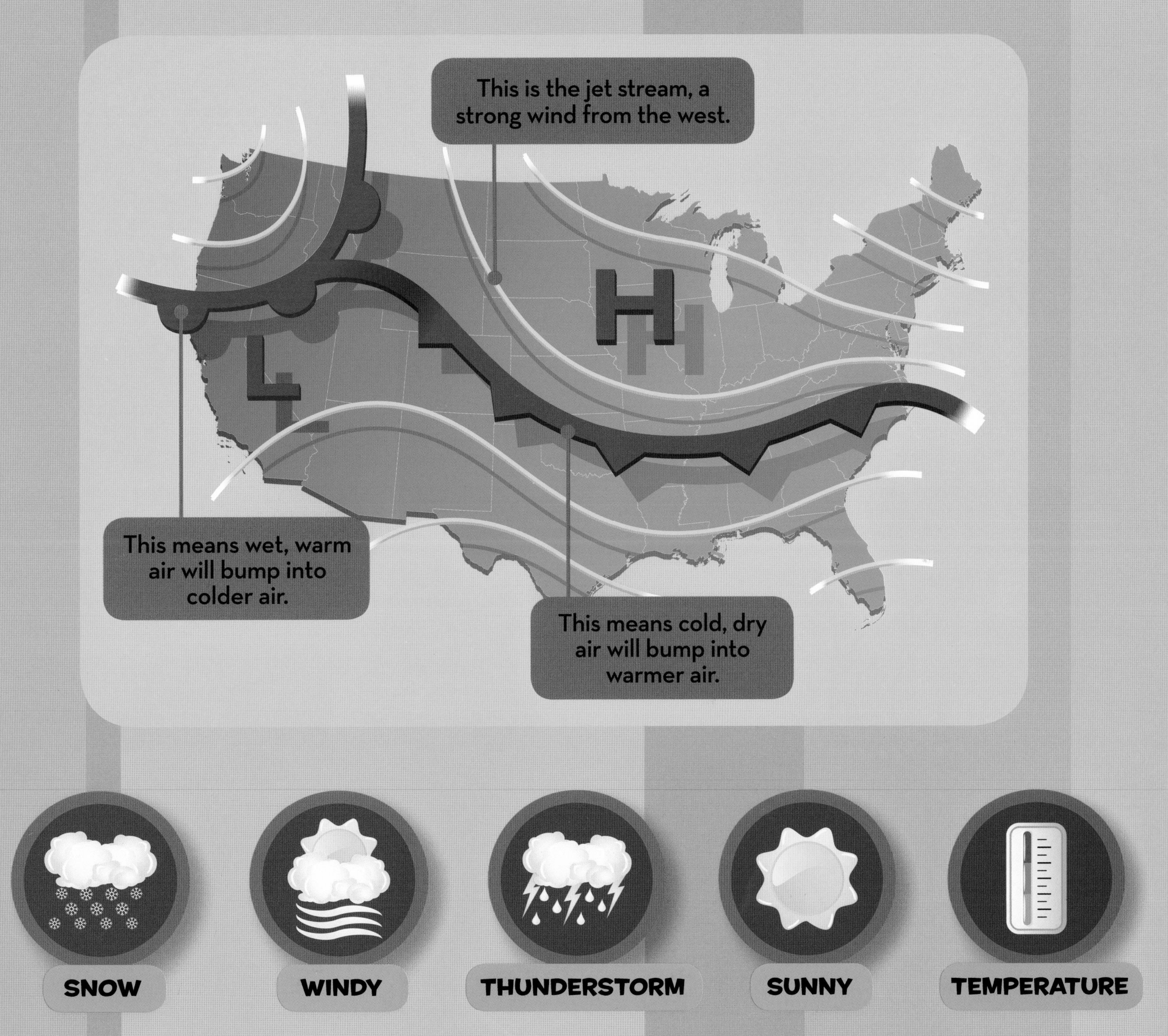
This is the jet stream, a strong wind from the west.
H
L
This means wet, warm air will bump into colder air.
This means cold, dry air will bump into warmer air.
SNOW
WINDY
THUNDERSTORM
SUNNY
TEMPERATURE

COOL WEATHER TOOLS

Meteorologists study the weather using sensors that measure the temperature, wind speed, moisture, cloud thickness, and other details.

Here are some of the sensors used to predict the weather:

A barometer measures air pressure, or how heavily the air pushes toward the ground.

NOAA

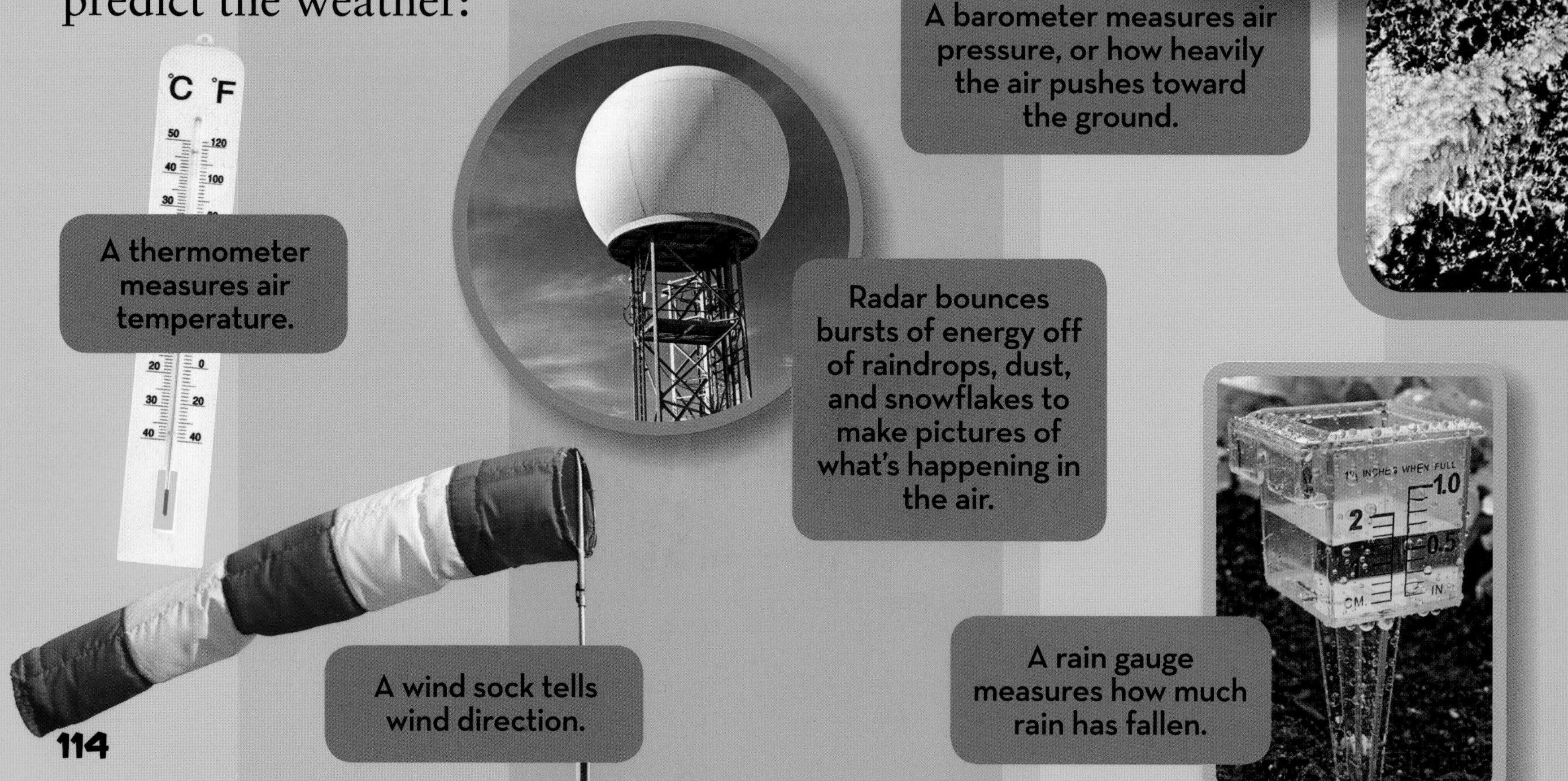

A thermometer measures air temperature.

Radar bounces bursts of energy off of raindrops, dust, and snowflakes to make pictures of what's happening in the air.

A wind sock tells wind direction.

A rain gauge measures how much rain has fallen.

A five-day **OUTLOOK** is a weather **FORECAST** for the next **FIVE DAYS.**

Experts can see that these clouds are shaping up to be a hurricane.

An anemometer measures wind speed.

What is today's weather like where you live?

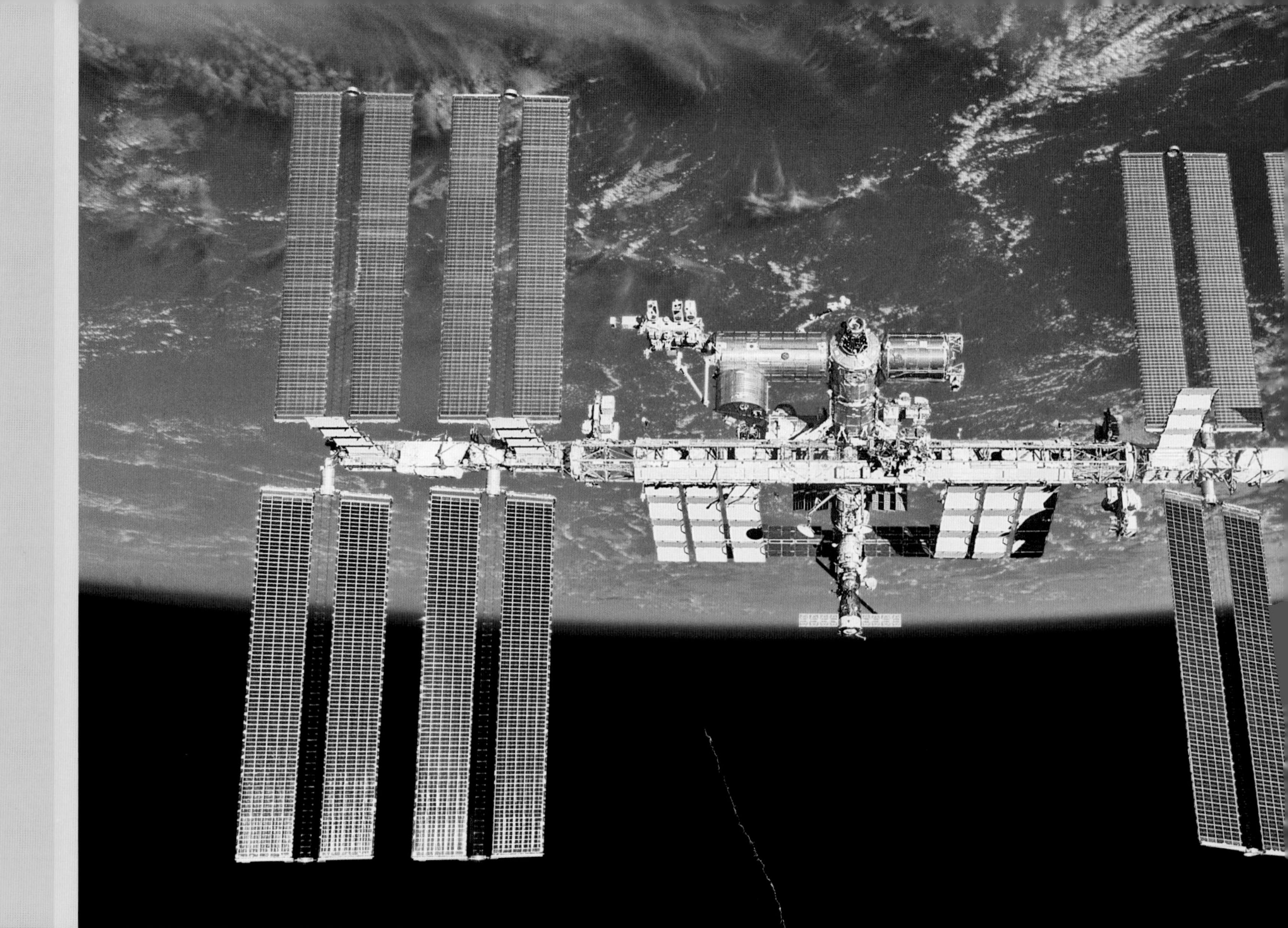

"EYES" IN THE SKY

Meteorologists use tools up in the sky to get information from high above the ground.

From 220 miles (354 km) above Earth, tools on the International Space Station help forecast weather by measuring ocean winds, dust, and pollution in the air.

Satellites circling 22,300 miles (35,888 km) above Earth take pictures of the clouds. The pictures show scientists the clouds' shapes and how they move.

POLLUTION and **DUST** in the air can **CHANGE** the weather.

A weather balloon lifts a sensor up to 20 miles (32 km) above Earth. It sends meteorologists on the ground details about air pressure, temperature, water vapor, wind direction, and wind speed.

THE BIG PICTURE

CLIMATE SCIENTISTS keep track of **ANY CHANGES** in the climate. They compare **TODAY'S CLIMATE** to records from long ago.

The weather is what's happening right now where you live. If it is raining at your house, it is probably raining in your neighborhood or city. But chances are it is not raining 100 miles (161 km) away.

The word "climate" is a way to describe the weather in big sections of the planet.

Some sections of the planet have a tropical climate. It is almost always warm there.

TROPICAL CLIMATE

POLAR CLIMATE

TEMPERATE CLIMATE

Some places have a polar climate. It is always cold there.

Some places have a temperate climate. It is warm part of the year and cold part of the year there.

What is the climate like where you live?

CLIMATE CHANGE

You have probably heard the term "climate change." It is not the same thing as a change in the seasons. The seasons change every few months. But climate change can make the seasons longer or shorter or warmer or colder than expected.

Many parts of Asia have a dry season and a rainy season. The change in the climate that has happened has caused the dry season to last longer. Without rain, farmers are not able to grow food when they need to.

When the rainstorms, called monsoons, finally come, climate change is making them much stronger. Very heavy rains cause dangerous floods and mudslides in many places.

MONSOONS

DRY RIVERBED

Climate researchers keep a close **EYE** on how our **PLANET** is **REACTING** to climate change.

Climate change is happening across the whole planet. The temperature for the whole year is getting warmer everywhere. Climate change is also changing the weather. It might get drier and rain less in some places. It might rain more in other places.

Nobody knows exactly how the climate will change or what the weather will be in a few years. You can keep track of your weather now. Then, when you are grown up, you can compare the weather to when you were a kid.

LET'S PLAY A GAME!

Using this map of the United States, describe the weather. Copy the pictures and symbols below that you'd like to use on a piece of paper, or make up your own. Cut them out and place them on the map to report your local weather or you can make up your own weather story.

Seattle,
Washington

San Francisco,
California

Los Angeles,
California

Phoenix,
Arizona

Salt Lake City,
Utah
Chicago,
Illinois
St. Louis,
Missouri
Dallas,
Texas
Houston,
Texas
Atlanta,
Georgia
Miami,
Florida
Washington,
D.C.
Philadelphia,
Pennsylvania
New York,
New York
Boston,
Massachusetts

PARENT TIPS

Extend your child's experience beyond the pages of this book. Get outside to play in different types of weather. Stomp in puddles! Build a snowman! Make a leaf pile! Together, you and your child can prepare for an outdoor adventure by gathering the right clothes and gear to have fun and stay safe. Here are some other activities you can do with National Geographic's *Little Kids First Big Book of Weather.*

KEEP A WEATHER JOURNAL

(OBSERVATION)

Keep track of what the weather is doing day to day, week to week, month to month, year to year. You and your child can describe the weather through words or pictures in a notebook. Write the day and date on each page. If your child has a friend or relative her age in another part of the world, help her encourage that child to also keep a journal. Then they can compare the weather in two places.

WEATHER WONDERS

(ARTS AND CRAFTS)

Make a snow globe with your child. Use a glass jar and a piece of paper that you can tape to one side of the jar. Draw a picture of a favorite place, object, or activity on the paper. Fill the jar with water and some large glitter. Secure the top and tape it shut. Then turn the jar upside down and tape the paper to one side, with the picture side facing in. Shake the jar and watch it snow.

OUT-OF-THIS WORLD WEATHER

(INVESTIGATION AND TECHNOLOGY)

Find out about the weather on other planets by reading National Geographic's *Little Kids First Big Book of Space*. You can also do an online activity with your child. Try doing a search for weather activities for kids.

YUMMY TREATS

(HEALTHY EATING)

Hot chocolate hits the spot on a cold day, but there are healthier choices as well. Herbal tea or hot soup warms the tummy in winter. When it's hot out, serve your child some frozen fruit to beat the heat! What other healthy culinary creations are inspired by the weather?

WEATHER READINGS

(MEASURING TEMPERATURE)

You and your child can use a thermometer to compare the air temperature in different parts of your house or apartment: the fridge and freezer, the laundry room, the kitchen, the bathroom. Then compare the inside temperature to the air temperature outdoors.

WEATHER WARBLING

(MUSIC)

Sing songs about the weather. "Sun, Rain, Wind, and Snow," and "How's the Weather?" are examples of songs that touch on the weather. There are many more that you and your child can find with a quick online search. You can also make up your own weather song.

GLOSSARY

AIR: what we breathe and feel all around us but can't see

AIR PRESSURE: how strongly air pushes against objects and the ground

ANEMOMETER: a tool used to measure wind speed

ATMOSPHERE: air surrounding a planet

BAROMETER: a tool used to measure air pressure

BEAUFORT SCALE: a measure of storm wind speed

CLIMATE: weather conditions found over one section, or region, of Earth

DERECHO: a huge windstorm associated with a thunderstorm

FOG: a cloud on or near the ground

FORECAST: a report of future weather

FROSTBITE: an injury caused by freezing of body parts

HABOOB: a huge dust storm caused by fierce winds

HEAT EXHAUSTION: feeling sick from getting too hot

JET STREAM: winds that blow from west to east

KATABATIC WINDS: very strong downhill winds

LIGHTNING: a flash of light and heat caused by clouds releasing electricity

METEOROLOGIST: a weather scientist

MOISTURE: wetness

SEASON: a period of time each year with particular weather conditions

STORM: a very strong weather event

SUN: the nearest star to Earth that gives off light and heat

SUNSHINE: heat and light from the sun

TRADE WINDS: winds that blow from east to west near the Equator

THUNDER: the booming sound that comes after a flash of lightning

WATER VAPOR: water as a gas that floats in the air

WEATHER MAP: a map with symbols that describe the weather in certain places

WEATHER SATELLITE: a spacecraft that orbits around a planet and can carry tools to track the weather

INDEX

CREDITS

Cover (UP LE), A.T. Willett/Alamy; cover (UP CTR), Pavelk/Shutterstock; cover (UP RT), Michael Durham/Minden Pictures; cover (LO LE), Barrett Hedges/National Geographic Creative; cover (LO CTR), Stocktrek Images/Getty Images; cover (LO RT), luchunyu/Shutterstock; cover (LE CTR), Christopher Elwell/Shutterstock; cover (RT CTR), scenery2/Shutterstock; 1, Ira Meyer/National Geographic Creative; 2-3, Gabe Palmer/Getty Images; 4 (UP), Erik Isakson/Getty Images; 5 (UP), FamVeld/Shutterstock; 5 (LO), Roberto Moiola/Getty Images; 8-9, M Swiet Productions/Getty Images; 10, Tatyana Tomsickova Photography/Getty Images; 11, Stocktrek/Getty Images; 12, Marti91257/Getty Images; 13, NoPainNoGain/Shutterstock; 14, Patryk Kosmider/Shutterstock; 15 (LE), Mimadeo/Shutterstock; 15 (RT), Sergioua/Dreamstime; 16, mekcar/Shutterstock; 18 (UP LE), Josef Friedhuber/Getty Images; 18 (UP RT), Moof/Getty Images; 18 (RT CTR), YanLev/Shutterstock; 18 (LO RT), FamVeld/Shutterstock; 19 (UP), Elena Schweitzer/Dreamstime; 19 (CTR), Katvic/Shutterstock; 19 (LO), Jahmaican/Dreamstime; 20 (UP), canadastock/Shutterstock; 20 (LO), fotomak/Shutterstock; 21 (LE), Ilyshev Dmitry/Shutterstock; 21 (RT), Jason Persoff Stormdoctor/Getty Images; 22 (LE), Silberkorn/Shutterstock; 22 (UP CTR), Nadezhda1906/Shutterstock; 23 (UP LE), wanphen chawarung/Shutterstock; 23 (LO LE), Ana Blazic Pavlovic/Shutterstock; 23 (rainy), Stephen Swintek/Getty Images; 23 (sailboat), Joshua Rainey/Shutterstock; 23 (snowboard), VP Photo Studio/Shutterstock; 23 (snowy), Borut Trdina/Getty Images; 23 (sunny), Ozerov Alexander/Shutterstock; 23 (swim), Jamie Grill/Getty Images; 23 (umbrella), Kinzie Riehm/Getty Images; 23 (windy), George W. Bailey/Shutterstock; 24, Patrick Foto/Getty Images; 25 (UP), Gregory Johnston/Dreamstime; 25 (LO LE), Kreatorex/Dreamstime; 25 (LO RT), Travnikovstudio/Dreamstime; 26 (BACKGROUND), ET1972/Shutterstock; 26 (bike), MNStudio/Dreamstime; 26 (boy), Karen Grigoryan/Shutterstock; 26 (flower), Czalewski/Dreamstime; 26 (girl swim), Kiankhoon/Dreamstime; 26 (mittens), Maria Chulkova/Dreamstime; 26 (sand castle), Nadezhda1906/Dreamstime; 26 (sled), Fotojancovi/Dreamstime; 26 (toys), William Berry/Dreamstime; 26 (tree), Sanit Fuangnakhon/Shutterstock; 26 (truck), Atlaspix/Shutterstock; 27 (beach), Vacclav/Shutterstock; 27 (boy swim), Luis Louro/Shutterstock; 27 (coco), Brian McEntire/Shutterstock; 27 (girl swim), Duplass/Shutterstock; 27 (glasses), design56/Shutterstock; 27 (ice skate), Tomsickova Tatyana/Shutterstock; 27 (kite), artpartner-images/Getty Images; 27 (skiing), FamVeld/Shutterstock; 27 (sled), Tatyana Tomsickova/Dreamstime; 27 (snowman), Lisa Thornberg/Getty Images; 27 (towel), Mike Flippo/Shutterstock; 28-29, Artur Synenko/Shutterstock; 30 (LE), Urric/Shutterstock; 30 (RT), Jupiter Images/Getty Images; 31 (UP), Fotosearch/Getty Images; 31 (LO), Francois De Heel/Getty Images; 32 (UP), Katrina Brown/Dreamstime; 32 (LO), oksana2010/Shutterstock; 33 (UP), Sanjeev Verma/Hindustan Times/Getty Images; 33 (LO), Patrick Orton/Getty Images; 34 (LE), Erik Isakson/Getty Images; 34 (RT), Dan Dalton/Getty Images; 35 (UP LE), tashh1601/Shutterstock; 35 (UP RT), exopixel/Shutterstock; 35 (LO), Susan Schmitz/Shutterstock; 36 (UP LE), Michael Svoboda/Getty Images; 36 (UP CTR), Flynt/Dreamstime; 36 (UP RT), Kreatorex/Dreamstime; 36 (LO LE), Astryda/Dreamstime; 36 (LO RT), Evgeny Karandaev/Shutterstock; 36 (LO CTR), Viennetta/Dreamstime; 36 (LO CTR), Juan Moyano/Dreamstime; 37 (UP LE), Cristiano Ribeiro/Dreamstime; 37 (UP CTR), Ronstik/Dreamstime; 37 (LO RT), Maxim Kostenko/Dreamstime; 37 (LO RT), Iriana Shiyan/Shutterstock; 38-39, De Visu/Shutterstock; 40 (LO), eleni/Getty Images; 40 (RT), Dann Tardif/Getty Images; 41 (UP), psychni/Dreamstime; 42, Barbara Ender-Jones/Getty Images; 43 (UP), Pecold/Shutterstock; 43 (LO), Dave Reede/Getty Images; 44, Alvov/Shutterstock; 45, Rob/Shutterstock; 46 (UP), Jim Cole/AP Photo; 46 (LO), megastocker/Shutterstock; 47, Barbara Ender-Jones/Getty Images; 47 (UP RT), Pakhnyushchy/Shutterstock; 47 (LO CTR RT), Scott Olson/Getty Images; 47 (LO RT), Jim Edds/Getty Images; 48 (UP), Scott Olson/Getty Images; 49 (UP LE), Volodymyr Goinyk/Shutterstock; 49 (UP RT), Alex Ciopata/Dreamstime; 49 (LO), Marty Melville/Getty Images; 50, cholder/Shutterstock; 51 (UP), Pal Teravagimov Photography/Getty Images; 51 (LO), Jim Reed/Getty Images; 52, Geddy/Dreamstime; 53, Mehdi Taamallah/AFP/Getty Images; 53 (UP), Joshua Nowicki; 53 (LO RT), Bennyartist/Shutterstock; 54 (UP LE), behindlens/Shutterstock; 54 (LO LE), Alexandru Magurean/Getty Images; 54 (RT), Malcolm MacGregor/Getty Images; 55, De Visu/Shutterstock; 55 (UP LE), Ralf Maassen/Shutterstock; 55 (UP RT), irin-k/Shutterstock; 55 (LO LE), tamara321/Shutterstock; 56-57, Alan Majchrowicz/Getty Images; 58, Ale-ks/Getty Images; 59 (UP), Andrei Kuzmik/Shutterstock; 59 (LO), wasja/Getty Images; 60 (UP RT), STILLFX/Shutterstock; 60 (LO LE), Anton-Burakov/Shutterstock; 61 (LO LE), CE Photography/Shutterstock; 61 (RT), aapsky/Shutterstock; 62 (UP LE), Inga_Ivanova/Shutterstock; 62 (RT), Anna Shtraus Photography/Getty Images; 63 (LO), Dennis Welsh/Getty Images; 64-65, phloxii/Shutterstock; 66-67, Stephen Swintek/Getty Images; 68, People Images/Getty Images; 69 (UP), Patrick Foto/Shutterstock; 69 (LO), schulzie/Getty Images; 70-71, Mike Grandmaison/Getty Images; 72 (LE), Darrell Gulin/Getty Images; 72 (RT), Coolekm/Dreamstime; 74 (LE), Roger Fletcher/Alamy Stock Photo; 74 (RT), Mimi Ditchie Photography/Getty Images; 75 (UP), Andy Rouse/NPL/Minden Pictures; 75 (LO), Quick Shot20/Shutterstock; 76 (UP), Pedro Pardo/AFP/Getty Images; 76 (LO), Karl-Josef Hildenbrand/AP Photo; 77 (UP), laurent/Getty Images; 77 (LO), Khin Maun Win/AFP/Getty Images; 78 (LE), Lars Lentz/Getty Images; 78 (RT), Image Source/Getty Images; 79 (UP LE), Marko Korosec/Solent News/Rex/AP Photo; 79 (UP RT), MimaCZ/Shutterstock; 79 (LO LE), Jason Persoff Stormdoctor/Getty Images; 79 (LO RT), Michal Ludwiczak/Shutterstock; 80-81, NASA; 82 (LE), Ross Tuckerman/AFP/Getty Images; 82 (RT), Willoughby Owen/Getty Images; 83, Topical Press Agency/Hulton Archive/Getty Images; 84, Jim Reed/National Geographic Creative; 85 (LO), Carsten Peter/National Geographic Creative; 86, Ryan K. McGinnis/Alamy Stock Photo; 87, NOAA; 88 (LE), NOAA/Getty Images; 88 (RT), Minerva Studio/Shutterstock; 89 (UP LE), Federica Gentile/Getty Images; 89 (UP RT), Thomas Backer/Getty Images; 89 (LO RT), Andrew Mayovskyy/Shutterstock; 90-91, Image Source/Getty Images; 92 (UP), Design Pics Inc/Alamy Stock Photo; 92 (LO), Barry Blackburn/Shutterstock; 93 (UP), Africa Studio/Shutterstock; 93 (LO), Ingo Arndt/Minden Pictures; 94 (LE), Sergioua/Dreamstime; 94 (UP), Sergey Kichigin/Dreamstime; 94 (LO), aphotostory/Shutterstock; 95 (LE), Sergey Kichigin/Dreamstime; 95 (LO), Henry Georgi/Getty Images; 96 (LE), aceshot1/Shutterstock; 96 (RT), FamVeld/Shutterstock; 97 (RT), Walt Disney Co./Courtesy Everett Collection; 98 (LE), Michael DeYoung/Getty Images; 98 (UP RT), Julia Freeman-Woolpert/Getty Images; 100 (UP), AF archive/Alamy Stock Photo; 100 (LO), Andreas Stirnberg/Getty Images; 101, Mahathir Mohd Yasin/Shutterstock; 102, Pavel L/Shutterstock; 103 (boots), NAKphotos/Getty Images; 103 (hat), Cookelma/Dreamstime; 103 (jacket), Andrienko Anastasiya/Shutterstock; 103 (LO RT), Josef Friedhuber/Getty Images; 103 (mittens), Andrey Armyagov/Shutterstock; 103 (pants), Miguel Garcia Saavedra/Shutterstock; 103 (scarf), subjug/Getty Images; 103 (socks), D_Zheleva/Getty Images; 103 (sweater), Ruslan Kudrin/Shutterstock; 103 (turtleneck), Kanstantsin Prymachuk/Dreamstime; 106-107, John Finney Photography/Getty Images; 108, Jupiteri Images/Getty Images; 109 (UP), Jeff Swensen/Getty Images; 109 (LO), Apic/Getty Images; 110 (LE), Romrodphoto/Shutterstock; 110 (RT), Josh Humbert/National Geographic Creative; 111 (RT), kenowolfpack/Getty Images; 112 (UP), Image Source/Getty Images; 113 (UP), Brandon Laufenberg/Getty Images; 114 (UP), Gl0ck/Shutterstock; 114 (CTR), pedrosala/Shutterstock; 114 (LE), Sergioua/Dreamstime; 114 (LO LE), Nickondr/Dreamstime; 114 (LO RT), Fireflyphoto/Dreamstime; 115 (UP), NOAA/Getty Images; 115 (LO), Kruwt/Dreamstime; 116, NASA; 117 (UP), Utah Images/NASA/Alamy Stock Photo; 117 (LO), NASA; 118 (LO), Stephane Bidouze/Shutterstock; 119 (UP), Denis Burdin/Shutterstock; 119 (RT), Florin Mihai/Shutterstock; 120 (UP), Santiago Urquijo/Getty Images; 120 (LO), idiz/Shutterstock; 122-123, Photoonlife/Shutterstock; 128, Lisa Thornberg/Getty Images

For everyone who loves to get outside, especially Cyane and Ellery, my in-house advisers, and John, ever the eye of any storm. —KdS

Since 1888, the National Geographic Society has funded more than 12,000 research, exploration, and preservation projects around the world. The Society receives funds from National Geographic Partners, LLC, funded in part by your purchase. A portion of the proceeds from this book supports this vital work. To learn more, visit natgeo.com/info.

NATIONAL GEOGRAPHIC and Yellow Border Design are trademarks of the National Geographic Society, used under license.

For more information, visit nationalgeographic.com, call 1-800-647-5463, or write to the following address:

National Geographic Partners
1145 17th Street N.W.
Washington, D.C. 20036-4688 U.S.A.

Visit us online at nationalgeographic.com/books

For librarians and teachers: ngchildrensbooks.org

More for kids from National Geographic: kids.nationalgeographic.com

For information about special discounts for bulk purchases, please contact National Geographic Books Special Sales: specialsales@natgeo.com

For rights or permissions inquiries, please contact National Geographic Books Subsidiary Rights: bookrights@natgeo.com

Art directed by Amanda Larsen
Designed by Yay! Design

Hardcover ISBN: 978-1-4263-2719-3
Reinforced library edition ISBN: 978-1-4263-2720-9

Printed in China
16/PPS/1

The author would like to acknowledge and thank Catherine D. Hughes, who has been a great guide for the writing of this book. A special thank-you to researcher Sharon K. Thompson for her invaluable help with this book.